Returns

John Welch

Returns

Shearsman Books

First published in the United Kingdom in 2024 by
Shearsman Books Ltd
PO Box 4239
Swindon
SN3 9FN

Shearsman Books Ltd Registered Office
30–31 St. James Place, Mangotsfield, Bristol BS16 9JB
(this address not for correspondence)

www.shearsman.com

ISBN 978-1-84861-932-6

ACKNOWLEDGEMENTS

Poems from this collection have appeared in the following magazines:
Snow, Tears in the Fence, Long Poem Magazine,
Blackbox Manifold, Scintilla, Shearsman magazine.
The sequence 'Yes Today' appeared as a pamphlet collection
published by Oystercatcher Press.

CONTENTS

Proses	9
Yes, Today	12
Without Title	14
Its Characters	15
Life Times	17
A Cure of Language	19
For a Grandson Aged Two	20
Park Life	21
Snatches	22
The Wind Harp	25
Enough Said	30
As it Was Back Then	31
Person	32
A Life of It	33
Her Testimony	37
Carefully	38
Returns	39
Morning	41
Limping	42
On Foula	43
The Visitors	45
In Camden Town	47
Jury Service	48
Gardening	49
Parked	51
The Silences	52
Someone	55
Born	56
Santa Maria Das Junias	57

Still Lives   58
Swan and Heron   59
Entries   60
Extracts from
    The Book of Breathings   62
Thoughtz: *From*
    an Abandoned Journal   65

PROSES

I read Modern Languages at Cambridge. Once a week we did a 'Prose' and a 'Translation'. We sat there, a group of fifteen or so, puzzling our way through it. No one said anything – no one, that is, except the person standing at the blackboard.

The Mairie

Chaque fois que chante
Son coq gaulois
　　　　—Rimbaud

Just up the road from where we're staying, in front of the faded Mairie with its pale ochre walls and bleached shutters, next door to the all-but defunct village school, stands the War Memorial, a black cockerel on a tapering plinth bestriding its heap of names.

Once one bit me on the lip. I was four years old and we were staying on a farm in Devon. It flew up behind me, that thunderous flapping as I ran, affronted at first and then terrified. My lip was marked with a shallow depression where the beak had closed over it – I saw it later in the mirror, the mouth's amazed contact with something quite other. Was this the cockerel that returned to me that night where I lay in bed half a mile from the Memorial? It was a waking dream at three in the morning; as if the bird were a helmet that grew from my head. The bird's beak and my lip seemed folded together, layers of bone and blood.

Yesterday the door of the Mairie stood briefly open as I went to post my letter in the yellow box. I paused in front of the wall to read the official notices posted there. These dealt with the hunting season, the delivery of permits, and with rules and regulations appertaining to the shooting of thrushes, larks and blackbirds,

birds of passage, water-birds, the use of nets and decoys. Lying in bed that night I saw them all again, this flock of torn and ragged bits of paper, and imagined them all rising up into the air. Passing by there again today I notice, between the two stunted lime trees symmetrical on either side of the building, a fledgling lying in the dust like an embryo fallen into the deep afternoon silence.

Segalas, Lot

Village de Malons

We'd been driving around in the pinewoods for some time. The sign at the turning said 'Village de Malons'. Here there were scattered houses and a wide grassy space. There was a P for parking and a sign for a public lavatory which seemed odd in such a small, out-of-the-way place.

We got out of the car. Complete silence. A vivid blue late afternoon sky, a stiff breeze and a few flattish bright clouds. We were quite high up here and just beyond the houses we had a view. 'Is that the Mediterranean?' you asked.

We turned back and went into the church. Inside there was a single candle burning. We walked about some more. We passed an abandoned house and, in front of it, a burnt-out jeep.

A young girl in shorts, a red shirt and a girl guide scarf came up to me. 'Est-ce que cette eau est potable?' she asked. Her voice sounded just like the water that flowed in a thin stream from a tap by the road and into a bucket, from which it spilled out into a broad stone basin covered in thick moss. 'Je ne sais pas. Je ne suis pas d'ici.' There were three more of these girls sitting on the wall opposite. Their faces were dark with tiredness and I wondered how they all came to be there. I felt they expected something of us – but it was too late now. Below the church and separated from it by a path was the graveyard. The door into it was locked and bolted. Such a depth of silence in there, waiting.

Walking back up, we passed the girls again. A middle-aged man was talking to them now. Tall and slim, wearing shorts, he was holding a lettuce. He sounded concerned, as if there had been some muddle. Just beyond them I noticed a house with a sign, 'Maison Forestière'. Was this where they were supposed to be staying? We passed a broken sign saying 'Restaurant'. I peered inside – a small dark room hidden away among all these trees, three or four tables set closely together and covered in check-patterned oilcloth. As we went on down the path I looked back and saw that an old woman had come to the door and was looking suspiciously up and down.

Well yes, it was like that, tasting this language, and always about to be fed.

YES, TODAY

When I dragged it this far
To pull it into the sun it was
A moment to be still.
There was no one at all where I fell.
Lost in you
Is the pause I fall into.

Sculpting what has been lost
You had left me a space in the air.
What's demanded of me, a random particle
Being just enough here to rhapsodise
Is to care for itself,
To negotiate unseen commands
Raising dark glasses towards the sun.
Words thicken into a braid,
A missing step   lurches me forward
Something to cover the place – a pen
Held upright, one like yours?

Leaving footsteps behind
To turn aside, ironist saunter
A bird's caught in flight
And shot clean out of the air.
An infant makes
Its passing sign.

Each morning starting to climb what I've made
The thing that pulls me apart is the thing that makes me.
The one true voice was the one that did not demand –
Was I trying to please all of you at once

which is why I wrote my name, just here
On the silence of a wall?

That paper trail layered with good intentions
Its almost extinct rustle –
What remains is more or less siftings.
A patient darkness falls across them.
I had shared out my voice
I can still hear its patient drone.
There's something that takes my breath
Being not quite what I had wanted to say
To the one I'd imagined
Poised on the lip of the wind.

WITHOUT TITLE

A dusty silence that inhabits me
It blinked at an art moment
But that sign become almost substance
Is it living or petrified?
Like alcohol's it's a promise never kept.
It will take me into its footsteps all the same
And now I am sitting here
In this silence, smoothing its hide.

But that text of his – unpublished
Where was its final resting-place?
Tempted by future gains it was
Something we almost believed in
Pages glowing with health:
We'll continue to research the horizon
Grasping at such brave tendrils.
Unkempt horizon! A masterpiece of sorts
Was what streamed past and could not be held.
But the substance of paper still
Where a book sulks in its binding.

ITS CHARACTERS

It's the white book of the sky
I struggle to mention
To know one thing from another
Being constantly taught the answer.
It was something left out in the rain.
All the same
This piece, it is like no other.

Cast out it's only
A short walk from here

With age losing balance
The words' spell

In whatever mirror you'll find it
But clearly stated

Perfected, this piece
Happened on, it is
An unreadable hieroglyph –
I brought back a series of glimpses

The book of the sky's
Imaginary characters
Each perfectly carved in pear wood.
'Ghosts building walls'

The dissolving art
Dissolves itself
And I can almost breathe, at last.
Being beside you now
I am close enough to be so far away
And each is only a fragment
Of what he had once written down,
Something thrown from an empty hand.

'Carved in pear wood' refers to a work by the Chinese conceptual artist Xu Bing titled The Book From The Sky. *The artist carved a huge number of imaginary Chinese characters from pear wood, the material traditionally used for this. The Chinese authorities objected to the work, using a phrase which translates as 'ghosts building walls'.*

LIFE TIMES

'I should like to have a book published and numbers of short stories ready. Ah, even as I write, the smoke of a cigarette seems to mount in a reflective way, and I feel nearer that kind of silent, crystallised being that used to be almost me'.
—Katherine Mansfield

M'other: Thoughtful milk
Being not-there is even more here
Language the stranger between us.

Meaning is you being held at a careful distance.
A buried voice endures
Bared voice, lonely armour.

In a turret of air I'd slept soundly.
Translated over a river of dark
I climbed down here from my piece of sky.
To speculate in the mirror.

Stay calm beside this water
Looking at beautiful people passes the time
Even so they are starved of their beauty already
Each stately and dying, a tree in a cage.
As you brush past the woman with the faded hair.
Give yourself time and you might become that reflection

Recovering from an illness
I scarcely knew I'd had I heard them saying
'Once we were alive and now we sing'
Escaping the mirror its sidelong look
In a small corner of the world, wrote

Far into the night to murder the language.
Figures of an impartial justice
Standing there side by side.

Ready to become
What I almost am
I'll sleep on through the brilliant afternoon
Above me's the blue of a patient sky –
The lips that cannot quite close, their perfect curl
A mute perfection.
'If I could have had two selves
Keeping one just for myself'.
And those poems? After an absence
I looked at them once again, just to make sure.

Having enough of what I lack
It's like being trapped in an airport for several years.
Publishing the remains
I get nearer to what the process maybe intends
An absence, embellished in the text
In a house whose unread books are silting up.
But the reader, where is the reader
This I being faithful to that other?

There are different voices have come to inhabit me now.
Hesitant I begin to talk to this other
Who is still there beside me. It is only a thought
Like the name of an unborn child,
Stand here one of the unfinished, waiting.

A CURE OF LANGUAGE

And as I live the life
This being one not quite doing it
Is what I like
The moment when it breaks,
Language as substance abuse?
It changes when it bleeds.
Most exhibitions are bleak little affairs.
As I said to the baby –
Taking the language cure
What did you find down there?
I forget where I just put it down.
Is it something that falls from the sky
Like rain that waits but doesn't quite fall?
It must have silent roots.
But still it hasn't found me.

FOR A GRANDSON AGED TWO

I pull the wine out of the glass
Like this. It reaches my mouth.

I was inside a lake
Its word spreading around me
A dry sound.

The water demonstrates drowning
The water imitates drowning
The water drowns

The two year old struggles
Mouth twisted into and out of shape
Word strangler. Like taking the blind for a walk
Something will fetch him and pull him away
Just so we are always being chosen.

Yes, the language can almost breathe you
This being lived in by another.
He kisses a mirror in passing
Someone might read the mark on it
It can't be helped, each smear of self.
Is it time for a final protest
A dry shoulder to cry on?
Else a dignity of saying
While kissing an error.

PARK LIFE

A lost task's art I do not wish it
Onto you at all.
Walking through the park
The eye still hungers.
Timidly gathered
Still holding on to our names
Here's one whose skin
Bravely wore its tattoos.
What answers when I speak?
What the sky delivers is just one name.
Praying and gaping
While broken bodies are carried past in procession –
This one he could have given
A meaning to the burial ground.
What you look at is what sees you
But waiting for it to emerge
Such vacancy, and lassitude
Cohabiting with other bones.

SNATCHES

In the destructive element immerse
                    —Joseph Conrad

Out for a walk words and phrases passing through his head
no pen, they blew away in the breeze.

Smoke rising from nearby houses –
The educated eye
Skyscrapers a distant procession

In the chorus of voices
Born out of stillness
Snatches

Bare branches on the sky
An emptied tree making words
The paper yields to a new supposition
Here it is printing itself
All over again.

'Face not recognised'
Touch the screen and remember
Each view, your self
Being endlessly curated.
Such careful writing his
It was a gifted silence.
A single bird
Caught flying into a mirror
They all went into the silence of the sky
'But I will be faithful to you
As ever is'

And today he can start
To be almost happy
Because his 'longing' is 'authentic'
Who went out to take a look,
Semi-derelict buildings
Little comfort there
Seeing that he is
The taste that ruin made
A sort of terminal exaltation. Today
He is trying to describe dust
Swept up inside him.

A city stores its silences –
The distance of those voices now
Plangent?
'I shall walk to the place where I am,
The wing of its distance
I might feel it brush against me'.

The educated eye, it roves
Its privilege reserves foreknowledge
Monotony of its breathing, enough
To forfeit the claims of air?
'They came and they saw'
Words trailed across the page.
Imagine the result
Somewhere carved freshly on stone
Where there had once been houses.

An educated eye
And the way the spaces
Moved about inside the painting.

The indifference that lives inside us
It widens its eye –
Perhaps there was less than he thought
Constructing an archive
While curating a self
Through lonely summers
The sunlight in his eyes? Well yes
It must have been somebody's idea
                                    Until
It was the page that silenced him

THE WIND HARP

Text Bridge
The text of a decent shame –
Don't look back at what's climbing
An invisible staircase dragging its broken wing.
It's inside you beginning to creak.
It bridges the sky.
Needing a mirror to make its silence in
An impure sanity of flesh
'This language, not my idea'. The book –
Who lifted a broken hand, the smell of its binding.

Beached
This man, this other
Whom brilliance of sunlight almost drowns –
He is a dark blur
Out on the beach inspecting stones.
So does he come
Foolish like this each day to stare
Drawn to an edge where there is no more edge?
Something there is wears out
As if a single look of mine might drown
That figure draped in sunlight
Till given a slight lilt
It disappears and goes inside
And I had wanted it so much,
That journey here past light-infected brickwork
The train a prolonged dawdle

Towards an absence nursed by rails, and now
This congregation of small stones
To say that, being here, you are
Almost word-perfect now.

Star Fish
Language the contract
Between self and nothing
When bending to earth it
Exchanges the sky for words

Out walking on that
Uncertain estuary border
Where we found the beached conger –
It was starting to swell

While gull-flight lifted over
Ocean   pectoral surge –
I walked there a neighbour
To that small ancient heart

Tracing the shallow architecture
Text an invisible lintel
Being lifted into air, then how it
Breathed itself away
Reached home my mouth
Turned inside out
Radiant shadow
Fabric starfish.

Drop Dead
No not that –
And it could be almost anyone
Just that it happens to be you

A first attempt
To banish someone watching,
Ink   the pens of others

Who's writing this? Not I?
But that relief being found
Each day's arrival with its slight reward

It's always there
A faintly irritating sound
Like wind-chimes from a neighbour's garden

Somebody out there
Who's in my skin   frail perch
Outside in the restless air.

Mask
This poor art wants to know, is the tightrope
You're walking on actually there?
The way it makes do with particulars
It walked a line and briefly
Failed to understand
Something his life tried to do.
It was the attempt as if he were shadowy bulk
Set against all that light.

The way a breeze introduced itself to the curtain –
Something moves out there
Like a voice playing with silence.
Mouth-heavy, she turns in her sleep

While beside her he breathes in that calm
Noticing age   Just soar
Autumn's dwindling
Arcades of sunlight
And now there is a faint
Upheaval in the air,
Bead curtain and eye-dazzle of broken lines.
Draw back the curtain and here he is, the reader.

Just A Touch
Such magnificent horizons are like an unfinished statement
Left 'hanging in the air'
And here they come with their carefully smoothed down poems
Multiple exchange of bodily fluids
That circulate in the economy of verse
The air full of broken branches
Was it meaning   that kind of
Lingering sheen on the surface of the thing
The game it played with itself
While we stood back and watched?
The aim of course, it was intercourse with shades,
Here at the edge the ex-fathers
In the shadow of words.
What the words bring is relief from absence
For a moment this sense of arrival.

The Thing About
it simply is
Where a statue is trying to remember itself
More and more is an echo perhaps
That waited around for an answer
'I didn't quite catch what you said.'
A performance of self?
It's using my words to remember the silence with
Till time walks off without me
It's something that makes a shape to remember us by
Only this time you are the event.
In front of a gold backcloth
The performers moved, slightly.
You turned to go and
Your pose was that moment
And it was the paint again
Like the sky all over your arms.

ENOUGH SAID

Is it because you were convinced the words were holding something back?

There are still sounds in the almost empty house
Page after page being turned
The pages now all at rest.

Forlorn script, pen is a word not a colour
All writing is imitation.
The desk surface ridged like the folds in a brain
He remembers lifting the lid and then
With a dip pen trying to indite the inkwell's darkness.

Too bright today's pages, alien reverence
The sunlight still at play
In the broken columns' shade.
Tenant of empty pieces of stone it is
Mere sign, so turn round saying
'Look at me now.'
Being filled with something other.
It settles him there.

AS IT WAS BACK THEN

Greeting the midnight hour the words surged on ahead
The white sheets blowing about, whose bareness filled with a
        breeze
As out and about went our voices drying off the surface.
Paralysis or trance? Prose fields shining with memory
But not sure how to detect the boundary
Between a voice and its murmur
Of sun-warmed flesh, its uncertain pulse of becoming
The day had no seam. I was the only discordance.
Now voices are hanging like smoke in the chill morning air,
Rustle of gravel below the window, as broken sleeps
Pay their homage to night, the daybreak reviewing
A reduced parade of birdsong.

PERSON

At the end of the day there remains what remained yesterday and what will remain tomorrow: the insatiable, unquantifiable longing to be both the same and other. —Fernando Pessoa

This weekend early morning's summer silence.
I should like to be in a different part of the city,
I think of taking the first bus that comes
To somewhere almost the same as where I am now.

Borrowing some of their air
I'll walk past the desultory front gardens
Imagine meeting another early walker
Who is always the same stranger.
Not knowing which of his names I should use
We shall exchange silent greetings –

There he goes, hurrying past
Pursued by his names.
I testify and testify he'd said
And ran into a different life.

Thought by another who thinks he thinks me
I'm still trying to find where he is
So that, written not in my name,
I could read him a challenge.
'You must agree to be somewhere
Dispersed into that various silence'
But this noise in my head, is it me
As I wake from a sticky afternoon sleep?
Nothing decided still.

Pessoa wrote using as many as seventy-five heteronyms.

A LIFE OF IT

The Artists

A dedication – to the ones who lead
Such interestingly selfish lives.

One Who

Yes, it was someone who said
I am a sour taste

There is nothing at the heart of it
But appetite and air

I and
I is
And would have liked to have my say.'

Biographies

In Paris back then
And 'No one to interfere with my art'
I wonder what became of him
And all the others.

Perhaps

Sighting myself
In that magazine – it was years ago
There was a community of voices
Perhaps. And I was, briefly
Part of it?

Spillage

Yes, poems
Poems
And more and more poems.

Submitting

      'I do not *submit* poetry'
You say you don't like them enough to publish them
Maybe I don't either
And that's why I sent them away.

Poetry Competition

The judges have all gone down to the beach –
'Now which is the best of these stones'.

Art Appreciation

Just keep on upping the dose.

Portrait Bust

The poet's
Head astray
Has settled here.

For Carl Rakosi

Sometimes, when looking at what I wrote
Back then and thinking, if only such plainness
As this man's here,
Who once went silent, before
Being summoned to speech again.

Visiting Hölderlin

'I asked whether I might keep one of these papers covered
with his writing' —Waiblinger

A long drawn-out agony of expense,
A moment of exile from the punishing voices,
Such dispersal of wealth among these dishevelled papers.
And his visitor records
When it is intelligible he always speaks
Of suffering, Oedipus and Greece'

And, to Conclude

Christopher Middleton's poem Without Shoes *begins 'One goes lightly / Down ignorant rays...' A researcher visiting the poet's archive in Texas found in there a pair of the poet's shoes.*

Unshod, the dark wood
Being lightly entered
All signs abandoned
The poet's shoes
Have walked him into an archive

An Aftermath

　　　　　　－ Half of the roof
Acanthus circle gone and the ceiling
So absurdly high it took a week to notice it
　　　　　　—Tim Longville 'Along Bohemia's Coast'

Along Bohemia's coast make landfall.
Maybe when the weather has eased a little
We'll hunt for them. Yes, gone,
End-stopped lives, a faltering.
I'm living in the aftermath already.
Back then a loosened line discovered
Needs I never knew I had, back then
When there was all that time
And always someone whose name went missing.
Until one day
This one came knocking at the door
Here he is, whose book smiles in your hand.

HER TESTIMONY

He used to come into that bar
When we were all drinking there and I'd leave
As quick as I decently could. He was always
Watching and listening. How his wife stood him
I just don't know. My god how I
Hated that man. In his book
There was lots of German, but he didn't know German
As I later found out. He was the first
Writer I'd ever met, and then frankly
I began to wonder if they were all like that.
He was cold. He had an affair with Carol.
He was always snooping around and then rushing home
To write it all down I suppose. My god yes I
Hated that man. He was creepy.

CAREFULLY

He laid a finger on the trees
But carefully, not one bird noticed
They went on singing
Exactly the same song.

He laid a finger on the sea
It went on rocking
Now harmless as a picture in a book

But when he laid a finger on her face
Her features turned to marble.
He turned from her
Walking away, down an avenue
Of fine upstanding trees.

Later she got up and dusted herself
Sighed, went back to cooking dinner.

He crossed the mountains a single night
He forded all the rivers with ease
It was his wish to be no more
Than a piece of paper, a coat on a stick.

Now that he's gone
The world rocks, like a picture in a book

RETURNS

An obscure desire to be somehow glorious
—Peter Schjeldahl

Remembering a time
When writing made him almost happy
The part of him he misses most?

This sparkle now, these clouds beginning afresh
Us in pursuit our hopes fanning out
Across future ground. Through many seasons
Trees branching out, and each one will open
A way out into the room of the sky
Where they will be talking about us.

Green windblown London at the end of summer,
Extraordinary returns among the loops of ivy
Through tunnels deep with brick, and then
A winged seed splayed on the wooden step.
Smells of an Indian restaurant, at ten to three
The street almost deserted. I thought I glimpsed
Stubbs' flayed horse in a betting shop.
Loudspeakers like the heads of horses
Brayed out results across the fields of paper.

Iris city with your humpback root
Proliferate in various dusty soils
Today is gusty with heat, like walking on plush
Lime trees filled with a low roar of bees
Then back to the house, overhearing
Piano notes rubbing their backs on the silence.

Sleep after lunch waits in my head
I wake to walls of pale sunlight.
Translating Baudelaire's 'merchant of clouds'
It's like lifting a plant from a grave, to follow
The one who was hunting
Apotheosis out in the restless street.

MORNING

First light. Not much to see beyond
An orange haze the streetlamps cast
But light will lengthen and a new and blameless air
Will enter even here.
Slipping out early to walk the streets
Is a brief escape, and now
The September sun's all-solacing light
Will start to explore my vacant room
Occupying an absence where
I took myself for granted.
Still muffled in their leaves the trees
Are a sort of motionless procession
A grey-blue tint. Out walking I contrive
To be outside all this,
Impersonal and quite detached
At full stretch of watching.
Until, my life being shadowed inwards
I shall come back, to get the piece of paper
I write this down on.

LIMPING

These peaceful afternoon torments, but now
I have a purpose,
It's winking in the glass.
But what's going on out there
I might have faith in?

Children are flying home from school.
I walk out comparing front gardens.
Here's alkanet, its vivid blue
A plant of waste ground transgressing borders.
Am I that dazzle hidden behind the trees?

Best to grow solitary, careless
Like this to hold on to each moment.
Maybe it's called fitful glory.
At four o'clock, lying down to sleep.
There was something I thought I might relax into
As an incomplete painting might almost finish itself.
Waking, wine stately in its glass
Runs dark between the pages.
But going out each day to make my peace
With something that I do not understand
I'll make a bandage for my wounded mouth,
Hide in the dazzle.

ON FOULA

Pray for our firm hearts to be orphaned
                    —John Wain

A small boat waited for us. And me?
I'm damaged goods being loaded up.
This was an island seen
So often on the horizon
A journey there might bring me
To a space where I belong.

Arriving here's an absolute
Refusal of the picturesque.
Brown or white, unshorn
The sheep seem dressed in rags,
A ruined croft's where fulmars nest
Tucked into corners, a feathered contentment.

Out on the cliff next day
I feel I am balancing on
A particular emptiness, below me
The fulmars, exulting in
Their sheer monotony of flight
Here I might escape into
The lightness of a story being told.

You in your particular distance
With pencil and with sketchbook
Were poised there at the edge.
And now you've gone out walking on the hill
While I sit in our sun-filled room
Watching a wheatear.

The energy of all this suffering –
My inner storms?
No, not suffering but moody angst.
I should like to make myself less,
Yes, to step free at last, just think
These creatures at one with their flight,
I could set out and join the rock down there
Being altered by all this air
Earthward not heavenward flying.

But you, you're out there still, and me
I'm watching for the sun
To fall on that bald distant hill again.

Shetland June 2022

THE VISITORS

Not breathing a word
The long grass is swaying in a wind
Sweeping towards you.

A house was a careful heap of stones.
Here we come, the tourist ghosts.
Yes, the doorways to abandoned houses
Where thistles are gathered,
Sheep skull on the window ledge
And our deliberations.
The going out the coming in,
Sunlight visiting the threshold.

The lochs so many
Pieces of upturned sky
Here is another, pause by its stillness
Just over there is its cousin the sea.

A tern's nine thousand miles of flight
Down on the shore
Is an egg laid among stones.

Out on an empty hillside
The chambered cairn has left us a scribble of stone
You lay inside it as if shamming dead.
Now it's the silence of my photograph
And the stones of the field we cross
Are a book I might make
But awkward to lift and carry

So carry on
Just walking walking meeting no one
Head foraging in all this air

Shetland June 2022

IN CAMDEN TOWN

She has this stripe she's painted
An inch wide, yellow edged with white
Running back from her eye
Along one side of her head, her hair
Stretched up into an enormous plume.
A summary skirt and fishnet tights
Her limbs all being
Articulate together.
Her leather jacket's torn, what covers it
Is something she must have done herself.
It has the appearance of writing,
Unreadable the dense deliberate scrawl.
It's late. I am all watchful hunger
As I follow her onto the bus
On a summer night when drinkers
Spill out onto pavements,
Night of the hidden reader
Who moves in a trance of watching.
I think is it being happiest like this
Always wanting to know what's written?
I could be part of every life and none.
There's a face that I could go on watching
And never tire of, gaze hanging there
Till it goes back to its branch like a bird.
Tonight I'll find my way back home
Back to my cube of light
Where I'll sleep, and waking early
When the first bird sings at five am
So single at that hour
I'll think I am its call.
Go back to sleep, until I wake up here.

JURY SERVICE

Where streets are laid out in a grid
Walking them, in an interval
And one small case to try –
The language back in there,
It curdled on my plate
In that room of padded drama
But why did the prisoner seem
The only one alive?
Out here it's Shopping City,
A half-disciplined army
And we have become
Introspective, among all these labels
While up in that kerbside tree
A bird tweaks stuff for its nest.
Then on to the school of drinkers,
Socratic kerbside band
The sunlight in their can
That has the taste of metal in it
And one small case to try.
Justice is still ticking over.
And marking time with pauses.
A bag of pronouns tied with string
Was shaken out, took flight.
'Please may I have the antecedents'.
Bowed back in there by a uniform
I feel I've been discharged
From something that I cannot quite recall
Being able to inhabit now
These spaces, civic and important.

GARDENING

Slow mover, walking up the hill,
A scent of wallflower. April's
A cold-hot cloud-bright Sunday.
In Harrow almost in heaven
A modest light shines on brickwork.
The mode here is mock-Georgian
Blood-red flowers on the rhododendrons
Cotoneaster's dull glimmer,
The dried-out beds of last year's leaves
And for those who don't care for gardening really
There's the modest-institutional mode
In troughs of concrete, soil like dried blood
The peat from defeated moorlands, ghosts of forests.

Her being alone whole days
Devoted to the destruction of weeds
Grubs hugging their jackets of earth,
Petrified cat shit
Grown inoffensive as soil, remembers
Dried flower arrangements spattered with silver
On a rosewood table's
Ghostly artifice of polish.
But how to disentangle
Imagination from death? She'll discover
Chaired in her hands a ball
Of fibrous matter dumped on the ground.

'The geums need tidying –
Those ones have turned out red'
Delphiniums, sprouting such baby softness of leaf.

Now a hot light sunders the trees.
Those over there look bridal
A gauze of leaves going on and on.

Moving away down the hill
As a breeze came to rest in the conifers.
There were faces screwed up against sunlight,
Soil sown with flint and pebbles.
A plant life is the one we aspire to.
Deeper than feeling the roots creep
Under the paving stones. Recover the surface,
With a small fork, worry the soil.
She gardens around a death,
Carries the weeds in gloved hands.

PARKED

The difficult afternoon
Grey sky, no rain for weeks, this trying wind
And he thinks of her holding sway,
In this suburb as it was
Back then and more than fifty years ago.
Everything's still pushing on from there
Like blossom from faulty trees
And her? She's almost here today.
More powerful her presence being withheld.
There is the wanting to get back to it,
The nothing-quite-happening of it,
Allure of lives held safely in routine.
Perhaps it was what was ordinary, but for him
It was precisely that
A world half guessed at, whose shining fabric
Had somehow edged away, and now
Today's these tired Victorian facades.
Whose people have a used-up look
And out here on his own
He's hunting for it still.

THE SILENCES

'Dr Wilson will see you directly'.
His eyes swim towards me.
I'd passed the shining, unused furniture
Mock-Tudor, mock-Victorian,
Crossing the leagues of lino, smelt
Its polish, recalling glimpses
Of playing fields, waiting all that time ago
An afternoon of Games
Smoke rising steeply in the quiet air
Just before the bell.

Yes, in the San and getting better,
Going out for a walk
With a boy called Rickards, I remember
This was a moment of escape
Although I'd no idea quite what it was
I was escaping from
Out in the softening springtime air,
Playing fields and woods, beyond them cars
That faded into far-off hills
And with them all the traffic of the world.

An afternoon too wet for Games?
Then exercise was walking
Up and down The Drive in uniform
The double shadowing my life
Moved somewhere just behind me
Whose silences were never to be told.
I stood there at the gate and wondered
Could that be my parents, turning in
In a hired black car?

Years later now, one windy sunny morning
The windows rattle, I'm
Abandoned in a dressing gown
Past caring in a sort of waiting room.
The other one is weeping.
Then I'm behind some screens
And someone brings a needle
Tipped with curare.
Her bland, incurious face above me
Is the last thing that I see
Before they pass the current.

Today's another splendid day
For wandering in those grounds
The monkey puzzle radiant,
In the breeze ferns swaying
Spores on the fronds' undersides,
A small wood on the hillside opposite
Patiently yielding to the axe.

Later there'll be Bridge for some
Downstairs in the library
Or you can borrow books
From the old librarian
Nodding there for half a lifetime
There's model-making with the therapist
In her dove-coloured overall,
A hot drink and then bed.
All the wards like dormitories are named
After our benefactors.

That convalescence over
I'd gathered strength for my departure
Leaving one winter afternoon
Carrying my suitcase
Limping away down the hill.
The lights were coming on
In the town as I approached it.
Did I dare look back?
To run mad in that interval
Had been my one indulgence.
As I approached the station what I heard
Was laurel bushes, leaves
Rattling behind me
And, typical of twilight,
The blackbird's hurried call
Somewhere among the rhododendrons.

SOMEONE

No the house was not empty
Not totally. There was someone there
Arranging flowers, dusting the tables
Preparing food. There was someone
Leaning over the banisters
Someone who turned to him, saying
'You do not know me at all'.

Outside some others were waiting
Standing beside their car, their faces
Bright with expectancy. But he went back
To his own face staring out of the mirror, back
To where the clock quartered the sighing hours.

Each day is like this now.
Each morning she brings him
His own head on a dish, staring.

BORN

A wish began at the threshold.
You loomed quietly over me.
Under the drum of your skin
Here is a moment that finds me. I'll join
His folded skin, its crumpled features
This lumpy bundle of cries
Half-seeing, who blinked, cried at the carnival.

Now I am stayed having kept my vigil,
Three o'clock and a seamless afternoon
Sleep, under those fickle eyelids, later
A kiss, the impending archway of a smile.
Life being just one enormous blur
He loans forgiveness to a shining world.
Born, his eyes fluttered the light
And now this steady all-encompassing stare.

SANTA MARIA DAS JUNIAS

A ruined monastery in Portugal

The part of me that waits to be alone –
I found it here, beside the living stream.
It was convenient as an ending
As if it were a bargain I had made.
You were not there to help me name the flowers
I could not name. Next to the church
Kept locked, used only twice a year
Was half an open coffin made of stone –
Boat or cradle? Disturbances of the wind,
The heat of the day, its burden of scents,
I walked back though a wood, trees thinning the sunlight
Out on the hills a wind farm lazily turning
And a stream's inconsequential dawdling.
All this will engulf me, but for now
There's something grows
Younger and younger inside me as I age.

STILL LIVES

To have such a body to breathe beside
Their endlessness together.
When he touched her tongue
The landscape was like an indrawn breath.
Entranced by the spectacle, further back
There was that infant held to the breast
Sipping the milk of oblivion,
The smell of a whole body
Its slow self-effacement at the hands of an emptying mirror.

Ground down the sand fuses
Into a mirror's glass
A petrified silence whose cold cannot tell you
How we dug at the sky with our empty hands.
Seeing a body exhumed
In front of our eyes
Here we are, again and again,
Thinking there is still time
To wrestle the stranger near.

SWAN AND HERON

This creature swung round
In its purposeful circle
Charging through the air.

Here just at the edge of the city
These wings were what I had looked for
And how they light up the sky

Heron, neck slender and dark
As a letter, turning its serif beak
Into the low October sun.

It is leaning so far forward now
Intent into the shining
Water of promise

Such fixity that gathers
All the kinds of stillness
Single-thoughted at the end of day.

ENTRIES

O and what I was trying to say
Just before you came in
But the words look tired on the page.
That's enough distance for now.
Remembering someone who'd turned away
From the loneliness of being human.
The obstacle I am to myself
Is a sort of life, to make the most of it.

Wanting to be as ordinary as earth
Here is a man with some sky on his hands,
Plinth, a man stepping off it and into the air.
The facade has satisfying columns
And all the things inside that are there to be looked at –
So much inexcusable symmetry
Where a flag empties the wind
As he goes on falling through a waste of light.

*

Older am I a parody of myself
Somewhere to hang these clothes? As if the flesh
Were talking in a voice I'd simply found
Out here perhaps, on the enormous sand
Sun sinking, flights of gulls. This time, I'd thought
I was not to be hurried home.
But here there's a siren sounds
When the tide is on the turn.
So, not to be caught on my shrinking island

I must turn back inland, towards a dark line of trees. That night
Sensed halfway to sleep there's a shadowy benevolence
On the tide's wrong side where it's done, a remedy of shadows.

*

Sagely nodding it was the day
They had finished moving the temple
A building covered in a shroud
Of honey-coloured winter light.
Stillness of the frozen air,
My being alone
With all the words I'd ever known
A single moment of light on a branch
Is the prodigal returning
So listen to me now – I'm almost here
A body seeking forgiveness wherever it goes.
One more time just taste the air.
Since it fell to me to write some of this down
On a day when the snow brought its silence into the house.

EXTRACTS FROM A BOOK OF BREATHINGS

Inspiration, after all
It's just a breathing in.
Outside on the street and looking up –
Sky rats? As over these
Fair gardens
Fractured dove sailed

HEADSONG
'We went in at the wrong angle'
                    The Brain Surgeon

Why is the lost head an oracle –
In mourning for its lost stem?
This self is an anxious enclosure.
Moments of such
Strangeness there are
The name of a once familiar street
I saw, high up on a building
That wasn't actually there.
I keep standing back from my life
Grazing its surface of meaning.
The victim I carry inside me
Who sleeps with poisons in his blood –
It's as if an almighty tune rose up
And I am being carried away,
On a pair of enormous wings
To a hinterland of the self, an enchanted orphan.
Here everything looks like a sign, the pronoun.
Slight as an inclination of the head
Being given time to breathe
All's in the throat, to gargle and sing
In too-close proximity to the language.

So took flight but caught by the ankle: for some days now I have been aware of a slight giddiness. Not an unpleasing sensation exactly, more a feeling that I might take flight, just go on and on upwards. I carry on walking carefully past people's front gardens. Look there's another wonderful oleander, and that's probably some sort of crocosmea. Is it the thing that's still in my skull that's making me feel like this? For now I'll walk home in silence, past all these interesting trees, wearing a mouth bandage.

We were this neighbouring reflection
What the dawn wind was telling the trees
You and I being the half of each other.
We plunge into it and survive
Like two strangers, each in our forest
With some carefully chosen pictures
Hung in our house. But the day
It has not quite finished with us.
It seems to outshine what we are.
As we sit in the garden and watch
How the sun at the end of an afternoon
Slants across. It dazzles the foliage.

Afternoon sunshine breeziness
All my days seem to be here at once.
Floating around the house, glancing at poems
Or out for a socially distanced walk
79 and carrying on
As if nothing had happened
Thinking I really ought to be happier.

Back home I take down a book of poems
It looks suspiciously unread.
This 'me' a floating article –
It is turning the pages for you.

There are two of us always in flight.
Full of each other and heavy
As our minds sink into.
An afternoon's giant yawn. After us
Who will be left, to superintend
This giant peacefulness of cloud?

Swifts criss-crossing the sky –
The first two years of life they stay
Always in the air.
When I found one out on the pavement
Like something the sky had discarded
It was otherness, distance. I carried it home.
Climbing a ladder I tried to launch it
An offering to the air.
It fell back. Impossible to feed
It lay there pecking at cardboard
Reduced to this squirming creature.
Next day it was still there
It had dragged itself over the grass, to where I stood.

Dusty angel –
Asleep under different eyelids.
Bird-life is so irredeemably other
But so close the stiff touch
Of a wing feather, moment of flight
Endlessly repeated

THOUGHTZ: from An Abandoned Journal

To go back to the beginnings of words is like imagining the skeletons of our friends —Elizabeth Taylor.

'He had set up a card table' I wrote, 'in the hallway, clearing a space among the boots and coats. The table was rickety, its baize surface stained. The children had put a box of sea shells on top of a chest and the marine effluvium coming off them combined with the dampness emanating from the coats hanging in the hall to create a melancholy effect. He had run out of A4 paper and was reduced to writing on the backs of earlier drafts. On the narrow window ledge in front of him he had placed bits and pieces picked up on the beach. There was a heap of quartz pebbles, a piece of what he took to be jet and, his favourite, a smooth flattened pebble of an unusual brownish purple with three irregularly spaced green dots. The disposition of these markings on the stone's surface must, he felt, be a sign.'

A breath that might animate the fragments, pieces of detritus but so carefully hoarded and watched over.

That place at the top of the spine, where energy collects, gets blocked, spreads back and down, creating all sorts of odd stiffnesses in other parts of the frame. To be more outside it, not always this pushing out from inside me, from the solar plexus.

A sprawl of language. Pulling the sentences away from you, like pulling a strand of chewing gum out of your mouth.

'Making art' – going out there, and bringing this back like something slung over a hunter's shoulder.

What is going on out there, something I might have faith in? .

So on to the museum: 'The deity's erect phallus, now lost, was made separately'. That tree trunk, it looks like muscle. Puzzling behaviour of crows and cyclists. Travellers weary with their baggage. A stateliness of trees, the grass all in flower

Uncorrected ecstasy. Kiss the sacred ground. Keep on kneeling.

This one, his 'reading problem' as if he lacks the humility to read because he is always trying to write something more. 'I'm someone who has just enough feelings to get by on' we'd heard him say. 'She'd rescued me from myself' he'd said, feeling comfortably exalted. 'I see less and less of myself these days'. Looking down the bus as he gets up to the top deck he thinks 'Now which one of you is the ghost?' Inarticulate He'll fantasise this 'other' somewhere out there in the city, a me-being-spoken. He guards these slivers of his misfortune. Meanwhile keeping himself from harm he hopes he'll have more to say. Thoughtful, meanwhile he sits there moulting quietly.

He can't help thinking what this text might have been, the phrases standing out there, in the chill winter air, at a point between remoteness and feeling. Now that the words are out there on parade they have the sadness of the unreached. What hangs in his mind is a possibility, this sense of a gap and what could happen in that gap, a place of freed words. He gives bits of himself carefully measured out and then he says 'I could not help bringing you this.'

Writing it all down deepens the silence. Dependence, a confused ache. A dream where I am ripping up sheets and sheets of paper, trying to get closer.

Mirror image, something that 'others' itself; a smiling mask that fascinates and this reader who, moving in behind you, hovers like an afterthought.

The only real me is the one that spectates all the other me's. 'And what would you not give for one moment of full presence?

'Finding yourself', a quest. Did you find yourself in a poem? What were you doing in there in the first place?

"What He Said" was what I said about you and me. And all the things I didn't say. But why did I put myself in inverted commas like that? There is no one here but myself, here in this pool. In that echo all feeling is laid to rest. Later it will return to me as a sense of strangeness.

There's the bit that appears just on the edge of slipping away when it suddenly 'works', an unexpected gleam. Coming as near to failure as you can, there's something you make that might finally relax into being itself.

What you have written down – you believe in it. But does it believe in you? The text – well, how does it look now? It's looking at you look at it – because it does look back at you. Like a wound, listening to itself. Now close your eyes and write down all you remember.
The watcher, perfected now, who slowly turns to face you with a statue's smile.

Beginning to write – all these new stars. Safely back in the future again.

These poems, when you started to write them, they came up to you, like half-guilty whispers from somewhere inside your head.

Maybe it is no more than how the parts simply lie there resting against each other on the page.

Poems crowded with things? Poems that move towards emptying themselves of things? Describing as a kind of devouring, something that empties itself inwards.

The words sitting down next to things, companionable alien presences. The sunlight's used look where it falls on a pile of books.

A restless night uneasy with dreams. Out walking first thing next morning I look up and there it is, a nest's frail perch, and I feel better.

This 'I' that hears me, an intermittent echo. Here's a mirror discarded at the side of the road, half-smashed, someone's reflection laid aside. Imagine walking into one, its blink of silver and that's that.

Wasting time, just letting it run through my fingers, not even trying to get anything done – what an indulgence. Something might come of it.

Dreaming myself awake and a hand grasps itself in the silence.

We fulfil our obligations while the real work goes on somewhere else in the shadows.

A world filled with voices is what we are left with. But somewhere the one true voice was the one that did not demand.

Something that a frame plays host to while outside someone is worrying away at a statue.

Improvising, on the edge of sense your words have outstayed their welcome.

Simply to gaze – an endlessly pacified hunger.

This flaring up, that stays here afterwards, an ash of colour.

Serving a meal in the gallery – this is her 'piece'. The cooling fat wrinkles on the surface of the stew. But who are these people waiting to be fed, each one looking anxiously over the shoulder of whoever they're talking to and asking themselves 'Who's that coming in now?'

Outside is the frozen park, unconcerned the sunlight like the rasp of a tongue on stone flesh. In winter when 'nothing' is worth the saying, a picturesque habit of lines. Spillage, a beginning. Fatal paper boat.

This swan's neck oil jar, Etruscan, its lip broken. Someone is brooding for ages over a gift. It has something to do with waste. Something forgives our ends? And the consolations of seeing, to outlast waste.

The words, if you could just get round behind them. Language, the other that occupies itself with you, is it inside you or is it somewhere outside? There's the catch in the text always on the edge of insurrection.

The way a poem projects its relentless knowingness all over the page, it was someone who said, I want to get out of here and into art What it finally means comes up to you and smiles. But inside you are shrinking away.

Paying your respects to certain forces – because the thing that pulls you apart is the thing that makes you.

An impure sanity of flesh.

Mouth-memories, and a particular mouth-music.

The feigned knot of a story

To be absolutely frank and straightforward and at the same time obscure. 'Written down' – think of it, the result as if freshly carved in stone

Each one its unreadable stone, surrounded by miles of nothing. To whom are the feelings due?

A performance: he means what he does, and you can watch him become what he is.
Then afterwards 'His silence spoke volumes'.

That moment when at last you find what has found you and it casts its sober spell

'Normality' a sort of optical illusion?

The cave, and the memory drink to the right of its mouth.

Moving into the 'city of thought' watched by thousands of defective cameras the eyes have it. The sun has just some out, the afternoon presses against the window. Be good to spite yourself.

Meanwhile, each footfall deepens the silence

Milton Keynes UK
Ingram Content Group UK Ltd.
UKHW040153070624
443686UK00010B/78